JUST... TRUST IT!

Jamie Taurima

BookLeaf
Publishing

India | USA | UK

Just… Trust It!

© 2021 Jamie Taurima

Presentation by *BookLeaf Publishing*

Web: www.bookleafpub.com

E-mail: info@bookleafpub.com

ISBN : 9789358361933

First edition 2021

MY FIANCÉ ROBERT

'Who I want to be when I grow up'.

You planted seeds in my mind only the strong can do and you loved wholeheartedly as you did it. You keep me curious about life and I love travelling our journey together. 100/100

FAMILY

Who do I admire? How does one put into words what family means? By speaking with actions, loving with understanding and expressing with kindness.

Mum and Dad, my sisters, my nieces, my nephews and my brothers, I love you all for who you are and the characteristics you all uphold.

Loving, kindness and loyalty, you give me strength, courage and have taught me gratitude

To the future and beyond! I love you

MY FATHER IN-LAW ROB RAPLEY

Success comes in many forms especially when it is combined with hard-work and love for all you do! I value all I have learnt and all that you have taught me even if it wasn't intentional. I hope one day I can stand looking with a smile and being as proud of my success as you with yours.

ACKNOWLEDGEMENTS

Aunty K, your guidance, support and love, there are no words! You loved me through some of my most challenging situations, and cheered for me the biggest in my success – You not only speak with words but your actions, which can move an entire city. Your loyalty and ability to bring alternatives to life is unexplainable and I will forever store your wisdom in my heart.

Friend, when I see you, I see a lady with so much passion for all she does. As I sit and admire all you do, my heart smiles with so much joy and happiness, you are a lady who chases all she believes in and I am so lucky to have been blessed with such an amazing friend. Chase the biggest dreams and watch it all piece together like a crazy 1000-piece puzzle. Coffee in one hand, lipstick in the other.

ONE WORD AT A TIME

Empty pages are all I see
Both hands shaking
What is happening to me?
Foot tapping loudly on my bedroom floor
Which route do I go?
Alcohol, chocolate or head for the door?
Like a game of frozen, I freeze
My mind is stuck
How do I flip it 360 degrees?
Raunchy romance or intensified crime?
Lift the pen to paper
Just start slowly
One word at a time..

CHAOS!

There is a replaying echo in your head,
Tears falling from your eyes
Words must be spoken;
Tears must be dried.
You now have chaos in your surrounding
Feeling broken, lost and distraught
Why did this happen
Where's the support?
Deep Breathe in, slowly breathe out.
Keep going! Don't stop!
Breathe in, breathe out.
Sleep, psychology, healing
Whatever you need to get rid of these feelings.
This is your time and you are protected
Fight your fight with no fear of rejection!

I AM HOME

My stomach starting to flutter like a butterfly
brushing your face
What is this foreign language I hear?
Where do I find this place?
It was a melody so sweet, a tune so tasteful
Simply like walking in the sand
The waves hitting your leg, ever so graceful
As I peek outside my window
To the shadows of the trees
I feel like this soul has captured me
Like an incurable disease
The soft sounding of the whisper immersed
within me so deeply.
Just like a caterpillar transforming
So confident and uniquely
My eyes starting to open
I feel my breath on my arm so lightly
I see a glimmer and I acknowledge
Thank you for guiding me home
Sweet and politely.

VALUABLE PEARL

A valuable treasure of sincerity
Her Innocence, wisdom and purity
Created naturally, strength like a stem
Gorgeous in colour such an elegant gem
There is 1 in every 10,000 to be found
Hidden so deep, in the ocean surround
Dress her up with any attire
Blue, black, yellow whatever you desire
She represents new beginnings as well
Tucked away in an Oyster shell?
Beautiful on adults or for a girl
Yes, this is her, a beautiful pearl.

FOR MY LOVE

Let me sit with you, wherever we shall go
Whisper your secrets to me
Relax and let it flow
This maybe the beginning
But I feel it's been longer
Your soul is so warm
Our connection, growing stronger
I want to learn your heartbeat
To understand you more
Not the dressed up, layers on layers
The deep, the hidden, the raw.
Teach me how your cup stays filled
Boilermaker, NRL, qualified & skilled
I asked for a man who I can love
For him to love me too
A kind, funny, hardworking man
How lucky, they sent me you!

THE UNIVERSE

Where do you find answers so clearly?
Or the warmth radiating your soul so dearly
Where crying out loud or being vulnerable isn't
a worry
Sitting in your feelings whilst repeating the
word sorry
Storage for your thoughts, feelings and
inspiring actions
Raises your frequency and vibration but first it
will remove the distractions
Acknowledge, Shift, Open
for all you really desire
You've done the work and your subconscious
mind approves,
Giving you what you require
Your path is now clear and blocks are being
removed
Depending on your values, belief and self-worth
The simple, answer for this is,
The Universe.

LIFE TO LIVE!

The moon is shining beautiful and bright
Sitting in the yard eating a Turkish delight
Extravagant, delightful, exhilarating
Keeping the soul at ease, so liberating
Peaceful sleeping through the early hours
Mountains, animals and abundance of flowers
Imagination can take us anywhere we wish
Living in sweet, calming, gorgeous bliss
You realise reality right now is like a dream
How you're living,
like a flowing stream
Mother nature has so much to give
Hold Gratitude for your life and begin to live

OUR HOME

Our home, A warm shelter built from sacrifice,
failure, success but most of all love,
by the hands of many involved
The Blood. The Sweat. The Frustration.
Our gratitude, forever. Our hands, ready.

Our home, features an abundance of colours,
materials and styles
Created and envisioned by us, for us.
The Zestful. The bright. The Limitless.
Our appreciation, endless. Our hearts, smiling

Our home, every dent, scratch and mistake you
see
Brings forward more of our personalities
The Rough. The Dark , The Distinctive
We welcome you, please come as you are.

EFFY, A MAN'S BEST FRIEND

She so calm, brown and loyal
Sleeping in a bed, caravan or on soil
She so beautiful and cheerful also
She gifted unwanted hair
cuddles and kisses more so.

It didn't matter if you were on time or late
She would greet you with positive energy
Effy didn't know hate.

Trips away everyone knew
Day or night in the car she travelled
Move over, Woohoo!!
His best friend is her,
She understood him heaps
His walk, his driving, his call
Never hesitated, didn't stall.

She ran to him so excited
"Hey dad I'm here, we are reunited"

Our home is nearly built now Effy
you're not here to see

You would love it oh so much
plenty of space to relax, run and be free

STELLA!

Wake up! Woof woof, please!
Dad, its 3am I need to run wild
Let me outside
So, I can steal socks, shoes and act like a child.
Please dad open the door, let me be free
Quick before mum wakes frustrate you'll see
I am black and white in complexion
mischievous, stubborn and I hate rejection.
I will cuddle and kiss you for days
Also jump on the bench or table, I am not fazed
I am learning to bark heaps, really loud
I love the workshop, I run there so proud
I wish I could roam and hunt for food all day
When everyone leaves, I get put inside to play
I'm so curious of what's around in the yard
My dad says
"One day puppy, you'll be a good guard"
I love my dad, he's a good ole fella
Yes this is me, and my name is Stella.

CREATIVE FLARE

One minute you're happy, next you're sad
You feel an urge come to surface
Making you question 'your true purpose'
Living a life everyone else desires
What is it that your soul really requires?
Some space for you to build your confidence?
Remove yourself from all the outside judgement
All the pieces will move into place soon
Meditate, find some peace staring at the moon
Sit write poems and enjoy the timing
Your intuition knows, just trust the timing.

OCEAN ROAR!

The ocean is giving out a loud roar
The waves are so huge and crazy
Watching it transform, so amazing

Warning people to stay away for now
No fishing, swimming, surfing or diving
Something has gone wrong somewhere
It needs to rest, stop people arriving

The clouds are covering the ocean
but you can still hear the waves roar
The kind of loud and heavy noise that hits you
right in your core

As the nights starts to progress you notice a
change in the ocean
The waves are sounding softer now
A big change in the motion

Thank you for your company ocean
Watching you transform has been grand
Nothing like feeling grounded and
watching the Sun rise
All whilst sitting in the sand

LIPSTICK AND EYELINER

What is it that I adore?
Is it the colour or is it the shade?
Maybe it's walking through
The Daylight parade
Could it be pink, orange or red lippy?
Dressing up in a tye-dye shirt, like a hippy?
Being amongst my feminine power
Acknowledging it, even if only for one hour
Dressing up, hair clips, make up and more
Letting my spirit speak
When I walk out the door!
Pitter patter, pitter patter
Off I go, embracing my energy
Where ever it shall flow

PONDER

Walking as I ponder
To the flowing water at the river
As I walk, I get a shiver

The sun is glorious and warm
Different to yesterday's mighty storm

Birds are chirping, the grass so long
Flowers so pretty, like a romantic song

I see a rock which looks like a seat
I sit down for lunch, to relax my feet

Everything seems so peaceful out here
In the distance I see a bunch of deer

No decor,, just so naturally styled
Living so carefree, free to run wild

WORDS SCATTERED

Something to make the heart, soul and ego
Really intertwine

Journals filled with brainstorming ideas,
making new creations

Spinning around on your seat leading to no real
destination

Without repeating the same language or feeling
stuck on a leash

For a newbie writer, what would you advise to
help them find their niche?

Cos this is the mind of a newbie writer
Squishing into a mould

Feeling like I'm stuck in the sand
Trying not to fold

WORDS, BE HARD TO SAY

You can show love in a multiple of ways
Love speaks in volumes shown by action
Visual and listening without a distraction

Mowing grass, laundry or cleaning
Love language, to leave the heart beaming
Another way to show your love language
Could be as simple as making a sandwich

There is no right or wrong way to care
Value, respect or add your own flare
Letters are a romantic initiation
To show them your loving dedication

Speaking huge volumes, deep into the soul
Or a simple gesture like going for a stroll

It is your love story, only you will know
How to express it, let it free flow

MOMENTUM

The past, a place of history
To think ahead, moment of mystery

We sit in our now appreciation, gratitude
Growing our self-belief, positive attitude

As our creative minds entice
Our self-worth, golden price

Flowing gracefully without resistance
Negative thoughts non-existence

Birds fly around us, flipping in the sun
Butterfly abundance making so much fun

Jade tree in the front yard -magnificent
Kids are playing, different instruments

So much to feel satisfied about
Not feeling icky, or stuck in a drought.

BIG WISHES!

Make a wish upon a star
A sweet wish of your choosing
Maybe you're wide-awake painting
Or possibly you're snoozing

Faith in your wishes
Belief in your heart

Like a story,
"Once upon a time"
Illustrated with loving art

You are your own artist
You make the story real
A house made of orange bricks, wooden blocks
or Steel

Just make the wish upon the stars
Hold on tight and believe until it is real.

SHE SCREAMS INTERNALLY

Sweet success is learning to navigate
through times and situations - trust
Could it be your star sign, cusp?

Good karma travels in a circle, no ends
Generosity meets gratitude- your friend

Meditating to find your peace
Ironing out the crumbled crease

To celebrate an internal win after a loss
Being and believing you are your own, boss

Let your success shine internal, so bright
Follow your heart to your destiny, alright

Your vessel is now open to see
Allow your light to flow internally